Finding Connections
Communication and Culture in 15 Scenes

Todd Rucynski

KINSEIDO

Kinseido Publishing Co., Ltd.
3-21 Kanda Jimbo-cho, Chiyoda-ku,
Tokyo 101-0051, Japan

Copyright © 2019 by Todd Rucynski

All rights reserved. No part of this publication may be reproduced, stored in a retrieval system, or transmitted, in any form or by any means, electronic, mechanical, photocopying, recording or otherwise, without the prior permission of the publisher.

First published 2019 by Kinseido Publishing Co., Ltd.

Design　　　　　Nampoosha Co., Ltd.
Video production　Todd Rucynski
Photos　　　　　TRUCZYNSKI, Tatsumi-san (photos of Mr. Rucynski)

音声ファイル無料ダウンロード

https://www.kinsei-do.co.jp/download/4076

この教科書で 🎧 DL 00 の表示がある箇所の音声は、上記 URL または QR コードにて無料でダウンロードできます。自習用音声としてご活用ください。

▶ PC からのダウンロードをお勧めします。スマートフォンなどでダウンロードされる場合は、ダウンロード前に「解凍アプリ」をインストールしてください。
▶ URL は、検索ボックスではなくアドレスバー（URL 表示欄）に入力してください。
▶ お使いのネットワーク環境によっては、ダウンロードできない場合があります。

CD 00　左記の表示がある箇所の音声は、教室用 CD（Class Audio CD）に収録されています。

Preface

Everyone is talking about intercultural communication and globalization but how can we train our students to think globally? The key is in the 3 C's. Understanding what Culture is, realizing strategies to Communicate those ideas, and then making Connections on a personal level.

Finding Connections follows interesting characters on an interconnected journey through 15 scenes that will present situations and language strategies to help students to make connections with those from other cultures. It is a character-driven book that also has a built-in teaching video of me in each chapter.

Speaking a foreign language fluently is not enough. There has to be a connection to the people and culture if one truly wants to understand the target language. Every culture has customs, humor, ways of thinking and rules of engagement that are somewhat unique. The idea for *Finding Connections* began years ago, in my efforts to help my students to understand, not just the English language, but also to provide them some insights into American culture.

The characters in this book are completely different from other books I have done. The scenes were true collaborations between the actors, crew, and myself. The situation and motivations of each character were decided upon but I never held the actors too close to the script. I wanted the language to be as natural as possible. The result, I hope, is a collection of fun and interesting scenes where the characters have been allowed to create something—true to themselves and their unique experiences of America.

The idea for the strategy videos came about for a couple of reasons. First, the videos are multi-layered. There is subtext that is just as important as what the characters actually say. This should be examined if learners are to get the most out of each scene. Next, there is absolutely a need for students to practice note taking. It is an essential academic skill that needs to be taught and practiced. The difference between spoken and written discourse cannot be taught without students experiencing it firsthand.

Finally, I hope the pleasure we took in making this book comes through to those watching. I believe every learner will find something interesting and exciting to discuss. Our goal is that this book can play a small part in helping students on their own journey in finding their connections in the years to come.

Acknowledgements

First and foremost, thank you to the Fluent Films actors because of your input, the videos are twice as good:

Jenny:	Chrystal Chau
Tim:	Nick Kowalzyck
Alex:	Sarah Moliski
Vinh:	Nhan Du
Maya:	Lipica Shah
Zac:	Austin Mitchell
Lily:	Caitin Mehner
Heather:	Arami Malaise
Kate:	Rachel Kaplove
Josh:	Josh Beyers
Max	Matt Dumont

I'd like to thank Ted Kerley, Jerry Caraccioli, and Simon in Morocco for all the logistical support. You made your homes our homes.

Next, to the Fluent Films crew: Eri Togami who also appears in 2 videos as "woman in the room." Arami Malaise, script supervisor extraordinaire, and Sarah Moliski who pulled double duty more than once, acting and as production assistant on the same day. Finally, to the indefatigable Jenny P.L. Tatsumi, who had more roles than I can mention. From makeup, lighting, catering, and shooting to name a few—you always gave it your all. Thank you from the bottom of my heart.

Thank you to the City of New York. There is usually no place else I'd rather be.

Last but not least, the team at Kinseido. I remember the first night I pitched *Finding Connections* to Nishida-san and Imakado-san. To my surprise, they liked the idea as much as I did. I am particulary indebted to Imakado-san though, without his guidance and patience, this project would never have been possible.

Todd Rucynski

Unit Overview

 ## Warm-up: Survey / Ranking

Ranking is a quick and easy way to activate learners and get them introduced to the theme. The hope is that conversation will follow. Examples are provided to help.

 ## Reading

A short reading of the same theme follows vocabulary and points of view will differ from the video segment. Questions follow to elicit opinions.

 ## Let's Watch!

Only the first half of the video is shown so that students can learn to listen actively and predict what will come next.

What did you hear?

After reading the 3 questions, students will find chosen lines of exactly what each character has said. This should lead to some grammar discussion as well as only one answer is possible in the given context.

 ## Let's Watch!

Learners will watch the second half of the video here.

Before Watching: Predict!

Learners will read the possible answers and predict, based on what they have learned about the characters and situation in the first half.

Watch Again: Pop-up questions

Here we watch the whole video. Four questions will pop up onto the screen. The questions are more in-depth and the challenge for the learners is to have remembered what they saw in the first viewing.

> **What do you think?**

This is an opportunity for students to voice their opinions on the theme and video.

Strategies for Improving Communication

This is a note-taking exercise that also reviews the video situation and offers advice and strategies for improving communication.

> **Strategies: Note-taking**

The first thing you realize when trying to take notes is that spoken language is different from written. The tongue is much faster than the hand. You can, however, learn certain techniques to write more quickly. To do this, you will have to make a system of abbreviations or symbols that you understand. You do not have to learn a set system. You can make your own but here are some ideas:

Using symbols. These are common words and most you are familiar with the symbols because of your keyboard.

    & = and   w/o = without
    ? = question   b/c = because
    % = percent   @ = at
    w/ = with

Standard abbreviations

    ie = in other words
    eg = example

Using only the first syllable of the word or leaving out final letters.

    con = conservative   max = maximum
    imp = important   intro = introduction
    ind = individual

Tips to remember:

Start with a fresh sheet of paper. You want to make sure you have enough space.

Do not try to write everything. Listen for discourse markers and words that are stressed. Todd will usually say, 1st, 2nd, 3rd, to help break down the information. Listen for facts, dates, and key ideas and underline the most important.

Check your notes soon after the lecture is finished so you can fill in parts you do not understand.

Strategies in Action

This is a time to practice the strategies with a partner or group. Students are given tips and, with all the other language learned in the unit, will be able to converse about the theme. This is the biggest step to finding connections!

Finding Connections
Communication and Culture in 15 Scenes

Contents

Scene	Title	Page
Scene 1	What made you who you are?	12
Scene 2	What is good about you?	18
Scene 3	Can you tell me about music?	24
Scene 4	When do you ask for advice?	30
Scene 5	Are you easy to live with?	36
Scene 6	What is your type?	42
Scene 7	How do you feel about compliments?	48

Scene 8	Do you like me?!	54
Scene 9	Can you guess?	60
Scene 10	Can we work it out?	66
Scene 11	How do you describe events?	72
Scene 12	What are you into?	78
Scene 13	How do you help a friend?	84
Scene 14	What are you talking about?	90
Scene 15	Can you tell me a story?	96

Character Profiles

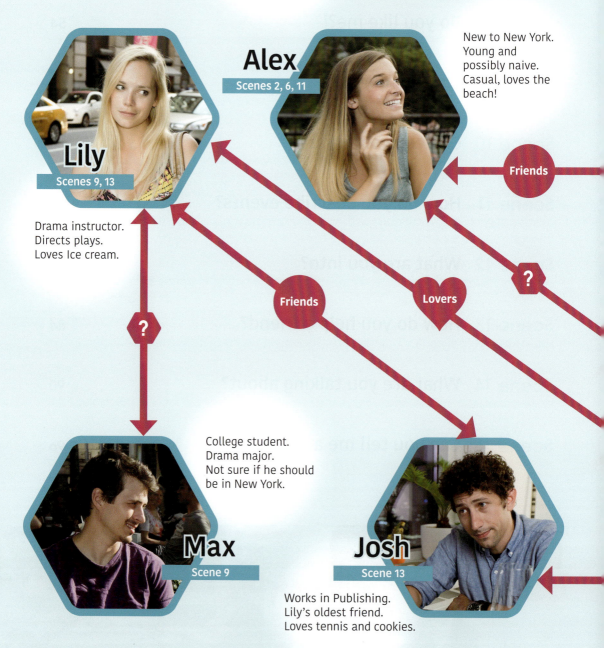

Heather — Scenes 3, 7
Music Lover, Photographer. Fan of Tim's old movies.

Alex — Scenes 2, 6, 11
New to New York. Young and possibly naive. Casual, loves the beach!

Lily — Scenes 9, 13
Drama instructor. Directs plays. Loves Ice cream.

Max — Scene 9
College student. Drama major. Not sure if he should be in New York.

Josh — Scene 13
Works in Publishing. Lily's oldest friend. Loves tennis and cookies.

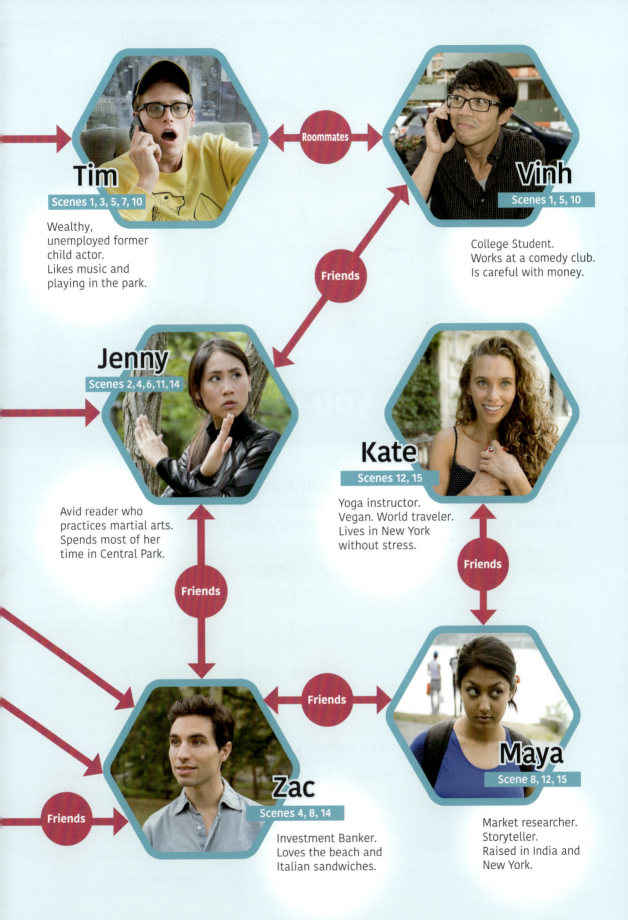

Scene 1

What made you who you are?

⬡ Warm-up: Survey / Ranking

🔴 **Rank how knowledgeable you are about your country on a scale of 1 to 5.**

	NO ———————— YES
I know the culture.	1 — 2 — 3 — 4 — 5
I know the food.	1 — 2 — 3 — 4 — 5
I know the history.	1 — 2 — 3 — 4 — 5
I am patriotic.	1 — 2 — 3 — 4 — 5
I know what makes it unique.	1 — 2 — 3 — 4 — 5

🔴 **Now share your ideas with a partner using the examples below.**

- I think I am very patriotic because I love the _____ and I can tell you what makes my country _____ in the world. For example, _____ and _____.

- I do not consider myself an expert on history. All I know is the _____.

Tips history / food / people / culture / politics / manners / customs / unique

Reading

Read the following text.

What does it mean to be Japanese or American?

What does it mean to be Japanese or American? Does it mean knowing the culture and history? Or is it only being born in a country and learning the language? Of course, the United States has a different history than Japan. United States citizens have come from all over the world. Still, some people expect Americans to look a certain way. What
5 do you imagine Americans look like? Many believe that Americans are Caucasian with blue eyes but this cannot be true for all if you know anything about the history of immigration in the United States.

The Gold Rush brought more than 25,000 Chinese to California in 1850s. By 1880, 25% of workers in the state were Chinese. More than 100,000 Japanese came to the
10 USA before 1900. Starting in 1975, 100,000 Southeast Asian immigrants per year, for 10 straight years, entered the country. These examples are just from Asia. Of course not all of the people who came to America became citizens but their children had something in common. If you are born in the USA then you are a citizen. Americans clearly cannot be identified by how they look.

15 Japan does not have a past defined by immigration but did you know that 36,000 children every year in Japan are born mixed-race? If they are born in Japan, speak Japanese, and study history and culture in Japanese schools, are they Japanese? How might they feel if they are treated differently only because of their appearance?

What do you think?

Share your ideas with a partner.

1. What are five questions you might ask someone you first meet?
2. If someone is born in Japan and speaks Japanese, do you think he/she is Japanese?
3. What would you say if someone does not believe you are Japanese?

Now, let's check out the video!

Let's Watch!

Tim and Vinh meet for the first time. Tim is interviewing possible roommates. They are trying to learn about each other to see if they can get along …

DL 03   CD1-03

What did you hear?

● **Choose exactly what each character says.**

1
A. I am a child actor.
B. I will be a child actor.
C. I was a child actor.

2
A. I'm sure it's how it sounds.
B. I'm sure it's kind of how it sounds.
C. I'm sure it's not how it sounds.

3
A. Me, too.
B. Me, neither.
C. Me, either.

What made you who you are? Scene 1

Let's Watch! 2

Before Watching: Predict!

● **Guess what the character will say.**

DL 04   CD1-04

A. I see. You are American!
B. So you grew up in New York State.
C. What's it like growing up in a village in Vietnam?

Watch Again: Pop-up questions

● **Watch the whole video again and answer the questions.**

DL 03~04   CD1-03   CD1-04

1. When and how old was Tim when he bought this apartment?

   _____

2. Tim mentions two movies he was in. What are the titles?

   _____

3. Exactly where did Vinh grow up?

   _____

4. What do Tim and Vinh agree on about Vietnam?

   _____

What do you think?

● **Share your ideas with a partner.**

1. How do you feel about the characters?
2. Why do you think Tim is confused?
3. Would you want to live there?

15

Strategies for Improving Communication

Strategies: Note-taking

Listen and try to get the 5 main strategies from the talk. Fill in as many details as you can. After, compare with your partner.

1.

2.

3.

4.

5.

> Now practice with a partner using the strategies above. You don't have to be yourself. Be a character. Have fun!

What made you who you are?   Scene 1

 Strategies in Action

🔴 *With a partner, do some quick research and find a country that you want to know more about. After choosing, let's look at the strategies and see how we can use them.*

1 Make 5 questions for a person from the country you chose. For example, "I'm asking about the national sport because I love sports."

> **Tips** Asking questions is a skill. Good questions have good reasons for asking.

I'm asking …	I want to know …
•	•
•	•
•	•
•	•
•	•

2 Understand your r_____ with the person. Are you meeting for the first time (job interview) or did you study abroad together?

> **Tips** Your r_____ is important to consider for the type of questions you will ask.

3 Acting fun! Pretend you are answering questions and choose a different f_____ e_____ for each one. See if your partner can guess how you are feeling.

> **Tips** Use posture and gestures to communicate too.

4 Imagine you are surprised by an answer. Admit what you do not _____.

> **Tips** Practice using the correct intonation.
> Really? / I did not _____ that. / Is that right? / I had no idea! / That is fascinating. / I had never imagined that.

5 Try making 3 more questions that border on the personal. Sometimes you are not sure how private the person is or if a question might be annoying. Personal topics might include: age, religion, politics etc …

> **Tips** I'm sorry but could I ask … / Do you mind if I ask about …? / This may be too sensitive but do people in your country …? / You don't have to answer if this is too personal but do you believe in …?

Scene 2

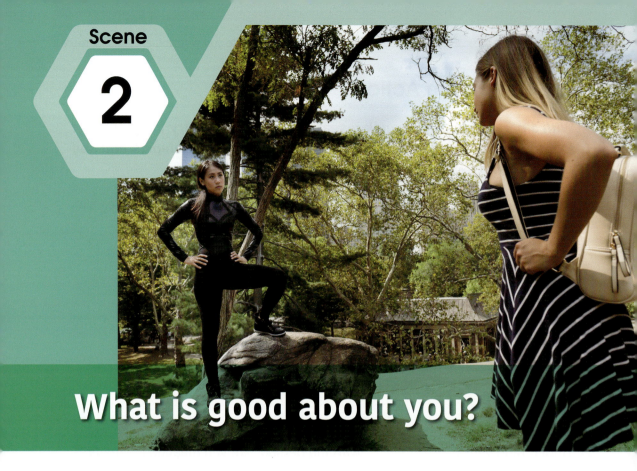

What is good about you?

Warm-up: Survey / Ranking

🔴 *Rank how you view yourself on a scale of 1 to 5.*

	NO				YES
I always do my best.	1	2	3	4	5
I have valuable skills.	1	2	3	4	5
I am more positive than negative.	1	2	3	4	5
I have goals.	1	2	3	4	5
I can solve most problems.	1	2	3	4	5

🔴 *Now share your ideas with a partner using the examples below.*

- I think I am a positive person because I am _____. I am usually _____ and want others to be happy.

- The world is a _____ place. It is not realistic to be positive all the time.

> **Tips** difficult / energetic / supportive / happy / smiling / friendly / hard / tough / strict / challenging

Reading

Read the following text.

How is your self-esteem?

Do you have high self-esteem? Is it something you were taught or something that developed over time? Not all cultures look at self-esteem the same way. The way you view yourself may depend on the country where you were raised.

In Asia, it is a virtue to be humble. This is also true in the West but confidence usually overshadows humility. Saying you can do something is the first step in doing it. So many children in the United States are raised to say, "I can do anything." While this cannot be logically true, it is a part of the "can do" spirit. It is a belief that trying is winning. Give it your best shot. The only way to truly fail is if you never try at all.

In Japan, even if you are good at something, people tend to downplay their skill. Someone is always better, so why would I say I am great at something? It is a much wider view of success but one that can make most accomplishments minor.

So which view is better? Americans tend to inflate their abilities but walk around with higher self-confidence and usually, the self-esteem that comes with it. Japanese, even if skilled, look at things from the perspective that there is always room for improvement, so boasting is certainly in bad taste. This may have the undesired effect, however, of lowering self-esteem. The answer lies somewhere in the middle. Why not understand that you have skills, and that you can always improve?

What do you think?

Share your ideas with a partner.

1. Do you have trouble saying you are good at something?
2. Is it better to say nothing, and just let others decide even if you are good at something?
3. What are you confident doing?

Now, let's check out the video!

Let's Watch!

In this video, we are introduced to Jenny and Alex. We find out about Jenny's background and her philosophy of life.

DL 07   CD1-07

What did you hear?

● **Choose exactly what each character says.**

1
A. I'm trying be a fly.
B. I'm trying to catch a fly.
C. I'm trying to fly.

2
A. No one was like me.
B. No one liked me.
C. No liked being me.

3
A. So, you aren't different?
B. So, you don't mind being different?
C. So, you are different?

What is good about you?   Scene

Before Watching: Predict!

🔴 *Guess what the character will say.*

🎧 DL 08   💿 CD1-08

A. I worry that people think I am strange.

B. I used to worry that people thought I was strange.

C. I never worry about what other people think.

Watch Again: Pop-up questions

🔴 *Watch the whole video again and answer the questions.*

🎧 DL 07~08   💿 CD1-07   💿 CD1-08

1. What is Jenny trying to do in the park? Why outside?

_____

2. Where is Jenny from? Be specific.

_____

3. What does Jenny read now? How about in the past?

_____

4. Why does Jenny read?

_____

What do you think?

🔴 *Share your ideas with a partner.*

1. How do you feel about the characters?
2. Why do you think Jenny is so confident?
3. Do you have any friends like Jenny? Could you be friends with her?

Strategies for Improving Communication

  🎧 DL 09   ⊙ CD1-09

Strategies: Note-taking

Listen and try to get the 5 main strategies from the talk. Fill in as many details as you can. After, compare with your partner.

1.

2.

3.

4.

5.

Now practice with a partner using the strategies above.

What is good about you? Scene 2

 Strategies in Action

🔴 *Interview a partner about the 5 strategies discussed and take notes.*

1. Play word association: Say a word like "SUMMER. SCHOOL. HOMETOWN. WINTER. WORK. TRAVEL." Your partner must answer in 3 seconds with an image. Are the images p_____ or n_____? Try finding the p_____ in all.

2. Ask about what s_____ your partner has.

   Tips I think I'm really good at … / I'm strong with … / I can do … / This makes me …

3. Have your partner tell a story about a friend.

   Tips My friend did … / I tried to help by …

4. Find out what makes your partner u_____. Have your partner explain.

5. The last part of the video says to have p_____. What can you do to get better _____? Jenny says reading gives her better p_____. What would make you look at your life in a different way?

   Tips After I traveled to India, I ….

Scene 3

Can you tell me about music?

 ## Warm-up: Survey / Ranking

● **Rank how interested you are in music on a scale of 1 to 5.**

	NO — YES
I listen to music every day.	1 — 2 — 3 — 4 — 5
I play a musical instrument well.	1 — 2 — 3 — 4 — 5
I often buy music.	1 — 2 — 3 — 4 — 5
I know the lyrics to many songs.	1 — 2 — 3 — 4 — 5
I want to join a band.	1 — 2 — 3 — 4 — 5

● **Now share your ideas with a partner using the examples below.**

- I _____ music. It is a _____ part of my life. I am always searching to try to learn something new about music.

- I _____ music. I listen to it but it is not my _____.

> **Tips** love / like / hobby / passion / huge / big / small

Can you tell me about music?   Scene 3

Reading

Read the following text.   DL 10   CD1-10

A musical connection

"Music gives a soul to the universe, wings to the mind, flight to the imagination and life to everything." — Plato

　　It can be hard finding what to talk about when meeting someone new. This is especially true when you do not share a common culture or language. There are
5 only a few things that can help you move past these barriers, and music, is one.

　　Music is emotion without words. It can transcend language and bring people together from different backgrounds. For many people, music is something they listen to everyday. It has never been easier to find new music and then share what you learn with your friends.

10 　　The kind of music you listen to often reflects your personality. Many people love pop music. This is no surprise because the meaning of the word is "popular." These days, popular songs around the world are not only in English. People in New York or Tokyo might both love a Korean song. This could be a great way to make a connection if you know how to talk about music.

15 　　There are countless other types of music besides pop. They are less common and so finding someone who likes a lesser known genre might be difficult, but when you do, the connection may be more satisfying. Remember, you cannot just say you like it, you have to say why. So go out and do some research and look at the history of music. Discover something new today!

What do you think?

Share your ideas with a partner.

1. Do you love music or is it just something you listen to sometimes?
2. What are your favorite kinds of music and why?
3. How do you learn about new music? Do you research or does someone tell you?

Now, let's check out the video!

Let's Watch!

Tim meets Heather in a playground.
He finds out how much she loves music.

What did you hear?

🔴 **Choose exactly what each character says.**

1
A. What do you listen to?
B. What are you hearing?
C. What are you listening to?

2
A. What genre of music is that?
B. What kind of music is that?
C. What kind of genre is that?

3
A. It's not so easy to explain.
B. Let me try to explain.
C. It's so easy to explain.

Can you tell me about music? Scene 3

Let's Watch! 2

Before Watching: Predict!

● **Guess what the character will say.**

DL 12   CD1-12

A. No, that's not true. I don't like classical.

B. No, that's not true. I don't like jazz.

C. No, that's not true. I don't like pop.

Watch Again: Pop-up questions

● **Watch the whole video again and answer the questions.**

DL 11~12   CD1-11   CD1-12

1. What 3 things does Heather say about "Slippery Mud?"

   _____

2. What are 5 kinds of music that Heather likes?

   _____

3. What are the reasons she does not like one kind of music?

   _____

4. Why does Tim say, "You lie!"? What is another way to say that?

   _____

What do you think?

● **Share your ideas with a partner.**

1. Why do you think Tim talks with Heather?
2. Do you think Heather is right about pop music?
3. How would you feel if someone suddenly asked you questions in the park?

Strategies for Improving Communication

online video online audio DL 13 CD1-13

Strategies: Note-taking

Listen and try to get the 5 main strategies from the talk. Fill in as many details as you can. After, compare with your partner.

1.

2.

3.

4.

5.

Now practice in a group using the strategies above.

Can you tell me about music?   Scene 3

 Strategies in Action

🔴 *Take notes and then present your favorite musician to a group. Make sure you use the strategies.*

1 Talk about the m_____. Is it fast or slow? Hard or soft? Melodic? Pounding?

> **Tips** My taste in m_____ is different from others/similar to most people. / I like catchy tunes like _____. / A lot of the songs are upbeat/slow tempo/ very hard/have a pounding bass. / They have 2 guitars/a grand piano/saxophones/ no bass player. / The singer has a fabulous jazzy/operatic/rock/bluesy voice.

2 Most music can be classified. What is the t_____ of music you like most? Find examples of 5 below that you choose. Choose some you do not know.

> **Tips** Rock / Pop / Blues / Punk / Classical / Jazz / Alternative / Rap / Dance / Techno / House / Heavy metal / Speed metal / R and B / Hip hop / Reggae / Soul / Funk / Trance / Disco / Electro / Progressive rock / Dubstep / Gospel / Ska / Indie / New wave / Grunge / Folk / Hardcore punk and more.

3 Talk about the l_____. Do they tell a story? Create a mood? Make you want to dance? Inspire you? Take some time to find your favorite song l_____. For example, I love the Chorus, it's … (tell the l_____)

> **Tips** Know the parts of the song: Verse, Chorus, the Hook.
> Styles of l_____: beautiful / poetic / playful / catchy / cerebral / raw / hypnotic / timeless / mesmerizing / moody / epic / dynamic and so many more!

4 Talk about the l_____ of the band. You can talk about hairstyle, clothing and make-up. Take a minute to pull up some pictures of your favorite bands and see if you can describe their l_____.

> **Tips** Most vocabulary is not specific to music. Adjectives like cute, cool, mysterious, and extravagant are suitable. Indie, Grunge, K-Pop, Metal, Goth, and Country have their own looks.

5 Do you p_____ music? Can you read music? When did you take up (instrument)? Did you p_____ live? Did your band have a concert?

> **Tips** play a show / play live / to take up an instrument / read music / to play by ear / perfect pitch / tone deaf …

Scene 4

When do you ask for advice?

Warm-up: Survey / Ranking

🔴 **Rank how you feel about giving and receiving advice on a scale of 1 to 5.**

	NO				YES
I ask advice from my friends a lot.	1	2	3	4	5
I ask advice from my parents a lot.	1	2	3	4	5
My friends always ask me for advice.	1	2	3	4	5
I always take the advice of my friends.	1	2	3	4	5
I always take the advice of parents.	1	2	3	4	5

🔴 **Now share your ideas with a partner using the examples below.**

- I always _____ my _____ for advice. I usually take it too.
- I do not like asking for advice from my _____. I need to find my own way.

Tips parents / friends / teachers / ask / tell

When do you ask for advice? Scene 4

Reading

Read the following text. DL 14　CD1-14

Advice—Choose the right path for you.

　Do you often ask for advice? If you do, who do you ask? This probably depends on the kind of advice you need. Asking advice is not just for young people. No matter how old you are, there is always someone with more experience or someone who can give you a different perspective.

5　Keep in mind that you can ask for advice and not take it. In fact, if you ask your parents and you ask a friend, you may hear two totally different ways of thinking. This is great because you can understand that people do not all think alike. It is similar to debate and you get to choose the path that is right for you.

　It may be beneficial to ask someone from the opposite sex for advice. After all, men 10　and women do not always think alike and if you are a man who wants advice about a woman, who does it make most sense to ask? There are actually scientific reasons for the differences. One example is that women have a larger limbic system in the brain which allows them to be more expressive and in touch with their feelings and emotions. This is not to say that men are not in touch with their feelings but why not 15　ask for another perspective?

　No matter who you ask for advice, the final decision is ultimately your own. You absolutely must try to get the best counsel, but it is your life.

What do you think?

Share your ideas with a partner.

1. Who do you usually ask for advice and why?
2. Do you believe that men and women think differently? Do you have any examples?
3. Do you always act on advice you are given? Have you ever gotten bad advice?

Now, let's check out the video!

Let's Watch!

Here we meet Zac for the first time.
He asks Jenny for advice about women.

online / video
online / audio

DL 15 CD1-15

What did you hear? ● Choose exactly what each character says.

1

A. Do you think that women and men can go out together and just be friends?

B. Do you think that women and men can spend time together and just be friends?

C. Do you think that women and men can share time together and just be friends?

2

A. I eat the foods you eat and I read books.

B. I don't think I eat any of the foods you eat and I watch movies.

C. I don't think I eat any of the foods you eat and I read books.

3

A. I'm asking you out. I'm not asking your advice.

B. I'm not asking you out. I'm just asking your advice.

C. I'm just asking you out. I'm just asking your advice.

When do you ask for advice? Scene 4

Let's Watch! 2

Before Watching: Predict!

● **Guess what the character will say.**

A. I do think males and females can spend time together if they share the same goal and if that goal is clearly discussed beforehand.

B. I do think males and females can always spend time together. It's just time.

C. I do think males and females should not spend time alone together unless they are dating.

Watch Again: Pop-up questions

● **Watch the whole video again and answer the questions.**

DL 15~16   CD1-15   CD1-16

1. What 2 things does Zac say are fun?

_____

2. Why does Zac ask Jenny for advice?

_____

3. What does Zac seem to want at the start of a relationship? (Hint: 1 word)

_____

4. Why does Jenny say she needs more information?

_____

What do you think?

● **Share your ideas with a partner.**

1. What would you ask Jenny advice about?
2. What do you think about Jenny's opinion?
3. Why do you think Zac does not give more information?

33

Strategies for Improving Communication

 DL 17   CD1-17

Strategies: Note-taking

Listen and try to get the 5 main strategies from the talk. Fill in as many details as you can. After, compare with your partner.

1.

2.

3.

4.

5.

Now practice with a partner using the strategies above.

When do you ask for advice?   Scene 4

 Strategies in Action

🔴 *Look at the strategies in your notes and fill in the missing information about advice.*

1 First, take notes about a time when you needed advice, had a problem, or had to make a decision. Take a memo below.

> **Tips** Follow strategy 1 and _____ to your partner.

2 You must a_____ q_____. Make sure and try to a_____ at least 5 q_____. Your input will make the problem clearer.

> **Tips** And then what happened? / What happened next? / How did you feel? / What did it look like?

3 Ask for c_____. Make sure you heard what you think you heard. Ask 3-4 times during the story.

> **Tips** Do you mean …? / Did you say …? / Let me get this straight, you said … / Sorry, could you say that again? / I want to be clear on this.

4 When giving advice _____ your answers as the strategy video said. Don't pretend to be sure.

> **Tips** It might be that … / It's case by case … / It's possible … / Do you think maybe that …? / It could be that … / Maybe you should … / I'm not sure but perhaps you should …

5 What advice did you give to your friend?

> **Tips** Maybe you should try … / If I were you, I would … / You definitely need to …

35

Scene 5

Are you easy to live with?

Warm-up: Survey / Ranking

● **Rank how easy you are to live with on a scale of 1 to 5.**

	NO ← → YES
I am easy to live with.	1 — 2 — 3 — 4 — 5
I can cook.	1 — 2 — 3 — 4 — 5
My room is usually clean.	1 — 2 — 3 — 4 — 5
I do not make so much noise at home.	1 — 2 — 3 — 4 — 5
I do not have any annoying habits.	1 — 2 — 3 — 4 — 5

● **Now share your ideas with a partner using the examples below.**

- I _____ a lot so I am a very _____ roommate.

- I play _____ so it can be _____ but is also _____.

Tips good / clean / play / drink / bad / guitar / piano / music / loud / noisy / fun / exciting

Are you easy to live with?　Scene 5

Reading

● *Read the following text.*　　DL 18　CD1-18

Roommates—The same team to maintain a happy home

　In the United States, it is common to go to college and be assigned a roommate. Imagine: one room, two beds, not far apart. A former stranger is going to know all of your habits, good and bad. At first it may make you nervous but it is often the case that your first college roommate becomes your friend for life. So how does that happen?

　First, roommates tend to depend on one another. If you sleep through your alarm, your roommate is the one who hears it. Don't do this every day or you will be really annoying. Other examples of cooperation may be shopping for food or cooking.

　Of course there is also a lot of communication. When you come back home it is natural to talk about your day to the person you live with, right? Knowing how your roommate feels about certain situations may broaden your perspective and help you to understand opinions that can be very different from your family members.

　Negotiation also plays a key role among roommates. When is quiet time? When should we throw a party? What time should the lights be out? How warm or cool should the room be? These are very personal decisions that must be negotiated when sharing only one room.

　Finally, roommates do not always get along. There will be disagreements but, more often than not, there will be a resolution. This is often where a strong bond is formed. Roommates learn to disagree but understand they need to be on the same team to maintain a happy home.

What do you think?

● *Share your ideas with a partner.*

1. Have you ever had a roommate?
2. How would you feel if you lived in an American style dorm room? What would concern you most?
3. What rules would you make as a roommate?

Now, let's check out the video!

Let's Watch!

Tim has a few more questions for Vinh to decide if he should be a roommate or not. Vinh tells his daily schedule and more.

online/video
online/audio

DL 19   CD1-19

What did you hear?

● **Choose exactly what each character says.**

1

A. What is your daily schedule like?
B. Do you like your daily schedule?
C. What would you like to schedule?

2

A. I'm a student, so five weeks I have classes during the day.
B. I'm a student, so five days I have class during the week.
C. I'm a student, so five days a week I have class during the day.

3

A. Did you join a lot of clubs?
B. Do you go out to clubs a lot?
C. Do you work at a comedy club?

Are you easy to live with? Scene 5

Let's Watch! 2

Before Watching: Predict!

🔴 **Guess what the character will say.**

DL 20   CD1-20

A. My classes start at 9, so I am ready by 8.

B. My classes start at 9, so I usually leave at 8.

C. My classes start at 9, so I have to wake up by 8 to get ready.

Watch Again: Pop-up questions

🔴 **Watch the whole video again and answer the questions.**

DL 19~20   CD1-19   CD1-20

1. What is Vinh's daily schedule?

   _____

2. How often does Vinh cook?

   _____

3. What time does Tim take a shower?

   _____

4. What does Tim suggest they get if Vinh moves in?

   _____

What do you think?

🔴 **Share your ideas with a partner.**

1. Do you think Vinh will be a good roommate?
2. What pet do you think Tim and Vinh should get?
3. Do you think Tim smokes?

Strategies for Improving Communication

online/video   online/audio   DL 21   CD1-21

Strategies: Note-taking

Listen and try to get the 5 main strategies from the talk. Fill in as many details as you can. After, compare with your partner.

1.

2.

3.

4.

5.

Now practice with a partner using the strategies above.

Are you easy to live with?   Scene

Strategies in Action

🔴 **Look at the 5 strategies in your notes and take notes about yourself. After you finish, you will be interviewed.**

1 What is your daily s_____? Talk about it in detail.

I get up at _____. / Have _____ at _____. / I usually take a _____ at _____. / I have classes from _____ to _____. / I work from _____ to _____. / I usually go to _____ at _____.

2 How much _____ do you make? Make a list of all the ways.

I play the _____. / I like to listen to _____. / I sing in the _____. / I don't make much _____. / I'm a very _____ person.

3 Tell how you feel about _____.

- I love the _____ of garlic. Many people don't but I do.
- Most perfumes are too _____ for me. I like natural _____, nothing too strong.

4 Do your _____ visit a lot? Who comes to your house and how often?

- I usually meet my _____ outside or at school. They almost never come to my place.
- I love it when _____ suddenly drop in. It's always a welcome surprise.

5 Where do you get the _____ for your rent?

- My parents _____ my _____ but I pay for utilities from working 4 nights a week.
- I _____ the _____ myself from my part-time job. I work a lot.

Bonus
Cover your _____. I'm not _____ but I'm not _____ either. I don't hate techno but I don't love it either.

41

Scene 6

What is your type?

◆ Warm-up: Survey / Ranking

🔴 *Rank how important first impressions are for you on a scale of 1 to 5.*

	NO ———————— YES
Looks are important.	1 — 2 — 3 — 4 — 5
Personality is all that matters.	1 — 2 — 3 — 4 — 5
I care a lot about fashion.	1 — 2 — 3 — 4 — 5
I have a certain type I like.	1 — 2 — 3 — 4 — 5
I believe in love at first sight.	1 — 2 — 3 — 4 — 5

🔴 *Now share your ideas with a partner using the examples below.*

- Looks _____ over time so they really _____ _____ very much.
- What a person looks like is _____. You ____ _____ a lot just by looking.

> **Tips** change / fade / improve / understand / tell / important / nothing / do / don't / can / can't / matter

Reading

Read the following text.

What if the cover had not been so attractive?

Everyone knows that you should not judge a book by its cover. But how many people have been attracted by an interesting cover, picked up the book and found it fascinating? What if the cover had not been so attractive? First impressions can mean a lot whether we are talking about books or meeting people. What is it that people notice when meeting for the first time? It is usually one of three things: physical attributes, style, or movement.

The first refers to whether a person is slim or more curvy, tall or short, sleek or muscular. Almost no one comes close to the ideal bodies that are found on the covers of magazines but there is beauty in diversity.

Style is a broad concept. It could be hairstyle, clothing, or even the way facial hair is trimmed. It could be how much make-up is worn. Each style sends a message. No make-up sends a message of being natural in America but in Japan it could mean lazy. Different countries interpret signs in different ways.

Movement is non-verbal communication such as facial expressions, posture or gestures. Again, these could be interpreted differently in different countries or even in the same country. A person slouching in class is generally seen as not interested, but is that always the case? The student could be sick and trying hard to stay and learn.

Are you aware of which cues you like and dislike? Do you project the images that you find attractive or is it time to make some changes?

What do you think?

Share your ideas with a partner.

1. What do you notice when meeting people for the first time?
2. Can you remember a good or bad first impression in your life?
3. What are you careful to do or not do when meeting someone for the first time?

Now, let's check out the video!

Let's Watch!

Jenny and Alex talk about types. Alex also explains her own style.

online video
online audio

 DL 23 CD1-23

What did you hear?

● **Choose exactly what each character says.**

1
A. Do you see looks or do you want personality?
B. Do you go for looks or do you go for personality?
C. Do you think looks or do you think personality is most important?

2
A. You can't judge someone by what they act.
B. You can't judge someone by what they look like.
C. You can't know someone by what they look like.

3
A. I think you can tell a lot about someone by how they dress.
B. I think you can tell a lot about someone by what they dress.
C. I think you can know a lot about someone by how they dress.

What is your type?   Scene 6

Let's Watch! 2

Before Watching: Predict!

● **Guess what the character will say.**

[online video] [online audio]   🎧 DL 24   💿 CD1-24

A. I don't buy designer handbags or brands. I shop in simple places.

B. I don't go in for designer handbags or brands. I like to keep it simple.

C. I don't carry designer handbags or brands. I like to keep them at home.

Watch Again: Pop-up questions

[online video] [online audio]

● **Watch the whole video again and answer the questions.**

🎧 DL 23~24   💿 CD1-23   💿 CD1-24

1. Why does Jenny choose personality over looks?

_____

2. Alex thinks you can know a lot about a person from clothing. What example does she give?

_____

3. What 4 things does Alex say about her own fashion philosophy?

_____

4. What do we learn about David's looks and personality?

_____

What do you think?

● **Share your ideas with a partner.**

1. Which is more important, looks or personality?

2. What does Alex mean when she says David was "OK"?

3. Are you your own brand? Do you agree with Alex that you can make yourself a brand?

45

Strategies for Improving Communication

  DL 25   CD1-25

Strategies: Note-taking

Listen and try to get the 5 main strategies from the talk. Fill in as many details as you can. After, compare with your partner.

1.

2.

3.

4.

5.

Now practice with a partner using the strategies above.

Strategies in Action

● *Take notes from the strategy video on what you believe. After, you will be interviewed by a partner.*

1 Why do you have the hairstyle you have now? What are you thinking when you choose your clothes? What do you notice first about other people?

- I like my hair _____. It's practical and easy.
- I prefer _____. I don't like being _____.
- I want to make a statement with my _____. People will get an idea of who I am just by looking.

2 Do you _____ in l_____ at _____ sight? What are your thoughts on the matter?

- I believe because it's happened to me. It could happen again.
- I don't believe in _____ at _____ _____. It only happens in songs and movies.

3 P_____. What kind do you prefer? What kind of person are you?

> **Tips** caring / independent / loving / strong / fierce / a thinker / easygoing / strict / hard-working…

4 V_____. What is most important to you? Make a list of your top 5.

1.
2.
3.
4.
5.

> **Tips** Money is very important. Without money, you can't do anything. / Love is on the top of my list. It's the only thing that really matters.

5 Do you have an image of your l_____ life partner? Write 5 adjectives describing the person.

> **Tips** I like men to be tall, dark and handsome. / I'm not into muscles. / For some reason I like noses. / I am not sure why …

Scene 7

How do you feel about compliments?

Warm-up: Survey / Ranking

🔴 *Rank how you feel about giving and receiving complements on a scale of 1 to 5.*

	NO ←→ YES
I often give compliments.	1 — 2 — 3 — 4 — 5
I receive many compliments.	1 — 2 — 3 — 4 — 5
I feel good when I get a compliment.	1 — 2 — 3 — 4 — 5
I feel embarrassed when I get a compliment.	1 — 2 — 3 — 4 — 5
I have a hobby that is my passion.	1 — 2 — 3 — 4 — 5

🔴 *Now share your ideas with a partner using the examples below.*

- It is _____ to give compliments. If I _____ something, I tell the person. I hope it makes the person feel _____.

- Giving compliments is not _____. I feel _____ when I get a compliment.

> **Tips** good / fun / necessary / strange / like / hate / happy / bad

Reading

● **Read the following text.**

Why not just be positive and say, "Thank you!"

People like to be appreciated. Compliments are gifts that are only given when someone finds it necessary. They cannot be asked for or demanded and that is one reason they are special.

It should be nice to receive a compliment, so why is it that so many times in Japan, compliments are deflected? Someone might say, "I love your new shirt!" only to hear, "It's not new. I bought it years ago and never wear it." If your friend is wearing it today, there must be a reason. It is probably because he or she thought it looked good. So why reject when someone compliments? Why not just be positive and say, "Thank you!"

It feels better when you are giving the compliment, too, if someone accepts it happily. When a compliment is rejected, the person giving may think it is too personal or something has been noticed that should not have been. I remember being shocked when a woman cried after I complimented her new haircut. She was not sad. She was very happy and later told me it was cut three days ago and none of her friends or family noticed. She was waiting.

Of course, it is important to avoid fake compliments. People can smell those from far away but if someone is giving extra effort or wearing something you love, do not hesitate to say. Positive energy is contagious and the good feeling could last for days.

What do you think?

● **Share your ideas with a partner.**

1. Do you like getting compliments? What is your favorite?
2. Have you ever made anyone angry by giving a compliment?
3. Do you often give compliments? Who do you give them to and what do you say?

Now, let's check out the video!

Let's Watch!

Tim finds out more about Heather.
He is impressed by her photography skills.

DL 27   CD1-27

What did you hear?

● **Choose exactly what each character says.**

1
A. You have your own style.
B. You have a style that's all your own.
C. You own your style and it's all yours.

2
A. I picked it up a couple of years ago.
B. I picked it out a couple of years ago.
C. I picked it on a couple of years ago.

3
A. So I just wasted how I felt.
B. So I just felt that would be a waste.
C. So I just feel that would be a waste.

How do you feel about compliments? Scene 7

Let's Watch! 2

Before Watching: Predict!

● **Guess what the character will say.**

online video　online audio　DL 28　CD1-28

A. My grandfather was the best photographer in the world.

B. Well if I didn't pick up photography, I'd have found something else.

C. I really feel lucky that my grandfather had such a passion for photography.

Watch Again: Pop-up questions

online video　online audio

● **Watch the whole video again and answer the questions.**

DL 27~28　CD1-27　CD1-28

1. How does Heather receive the first compliment from Tim?

2. Heather's grandfather had a collection of what 2 things?

3. What did Heather do so the collection would not go to waste?

4. What is Tim's passion? When did he peak?

What do you think?

● **Share your ideas with a partner.**

1. What was the key to Heather becoming a good photographer?

2. Why do you think Heather looks shocked when Tim says, "Well, that's fortunate!"?

3. Do you think it is important to have one passion or have many hobbies?

51

Strategies for Improving Communication

 DL 29　CD1-29

Strategies: Note-taking

Listen and try to get the 4 main strategies from the talk. Fill in as many details as you can. After, compare with your partner.

Giving c_____

1

2

Receiving c_____

1

2

Now practice with a partner using the strategies above.

How do you feel about compliments? Scene

⬢ Strategies in Action

🔴 *Have fun complimenting and getting compliments from your partner.*

■ Comment on a piece of clothing, hairstyle, or the personality of your partner.

Giving c_____

1 Find the right _____. Mean what you say and say what you mean.

Tips Amazing / Awesome / Beautiful / Cool / Fantastic / Unique / Interesting

2 Talk _____. Tell why you like something. Give reasons for your compliment.

Tips I've never seen anything like that before! / The design is really amazing. / What a fabulous color! / That fabric looks very comfortable, is it?

Receiving c_____

1 Say t_____ y_____ and add some information. Adding information will help the conversation to move forward. Stay positive!

Tips
- T_____ y_____. I bought it in (place). It was on sale.
- My hair? I think my stylist is really good too. She studied in London.

2 If you can't say _____ _____, you can try asking another question back to the person.

Tips Do you think so? / Are you sure? / Really, I'm happy you said so because I wasn't sure. / Really? That is very kind.

Scene 8

Do you like me?!

Warm-up: Survey / Ranking

🔴 *Rank how self-aware you are on a scale of 1 to 5.*

	NO — YES
I always know when someone likes me.	1 — 2 — 3 — 4 — 5
I can easily see when my friend has a problem.	1 — 2 — 3 — 4 — 5
I make a lot of eye contact with people I know.	1 — 2 — 3 — 4 — 5
I smile more than most people I know.	1 — 2 — 3 — 4 — 5
I text some friends more than 10 times a day.	1 — 2 — 3 — 4 — 5

🔴 *Now share your ideas with a partner using the examples below.*

- It is easy to see _____ someone likes me. I can tell by the way they _____.

- All people are different so I _____ _____ when someone _____ me. I usually don't know until they _____ me.

Tips when / why / act / speak / tell / do / don't / know / loves / hates / likes

Reading

● *Read the following text.*

How can someone know their relationship status?

Clarity is a priority in English. You should say what you mean and mean what you say. Japanese is more subtle. It is customary to take a less direct approach in discussions. In Japanese it is a given that you need to "read the air." There is, however, one instance where Japanese is more direct: confessing love. Too fast, too soon would scare off most Americans. So how can someone know their relationship status in English?

Unlike the Japanese who make it perfectly clear, a couple in America can go weeks or even months spending time together without stating intentions. The first step may be meeting in class and then going out for a coffee and conversation. Possible couples can do this numerous times before taking things a step further. Going to the movies or having dinner in a romantic restaurant is definitely a more serious meeting but it does not mean that the couple is officially dating until someone says something. It is even common to cook dinner at your home for a friend of the opposite sex.

Of course, there are clues just like in Japan. Some people say they know if someone likes them just by looking at the person's eyes. Or, it could be how close the other person stands next to you.

What needs to be understood is that there is a difference between the United States and Japan on this issue. Directly stating your intentions before a relationship has a chance to bloom would scare off most Americans. Meanwhile, not saying anything for months would surely leave most Japanese confused.

What do you think?

● *Share your ideas with a partner.*

1. How do you feel about the clear way that Japanese state their love? Can you imagine advantages and disadvantages?
2. Would you go to movies or out to a nice dinner with someone you are not dating?
3. What are the easiest ways to know if someone likes you?

Let's Watch!

Zac is concerned about a new friend.
Maya is happy to listen and give advice.

DL 31   CD1-31

What did you hear?

● Choose exactly what each character says.

1

A. I have a secret.
B. I've kept a secret.
C. I can keep a secret.

2

A. She was just trying to be nice.
B. It was just nice to be trying.
C. I was just trying to be nice.

3

A. It's so easy here.
B. It's not easy here.
C. It must be easy here.

Do you like me?!   Scene 8

Let's Watch! 2

Before Watching: Predict!

● **Guess what the character will say.**

DL 32   CD1-32

A. Why do you love the beach?
B. The beach is not New York City.
C. The beach is the best part of New York City!

Watch Again: Pop-up questions

● **Watch the whole video again and answer the questions.**

DL 31~32   CD1-31   CD1-32

1. Does Zac want anyone to know about his story?

_____

2. Who introduced Alex to Zac?

_____

3. Name 2 reasons why Zac decided to show Alex around New York?

_____

4. What 3 examples does Maya give Zac to understand if Alex likes him?

_____

What do you think?

● **Share your ideas with a partner.**

1. Do you think Zac is being nice? Why or why not?

2. Which of Maya's examples is most important to understand if someone likes you?

3. What do you think Zac should do?

Strategies for Improving Communication

 DL 33 CD1-33

Strategies: Note-taking

Listen and try to get the 5 main strategies from the talk. Fill in as many details as you can. After, compare with your partner.

1

2

3

4

5

Now practice with a partner using the strategies above.

Do you like me?!   Scene 8

Strategies in Action

● **Look at the reasons given in the strategy video. Take a memo on how you feel about each one. After, you will discuss with a partner.**

1 How close is too close? Of course it is different depending on the person. Where is the border and what do you do when someone crosses into your p_____ s_____?

Tips
- I move back quickly when someone gets this _____.
- I'm pretty accepting. I think my p_____ s_____ is smaller than most people.

2 How much e_____ c_____ do you usually make? In what situations do you avoid it? When is it necessary? Give examples.

Tips
- I tend to make a lot of e_____ c_____. I think it helps me to communicate.
- E_____ c_____ bothers me sometimes. It's too personal.

3 Do you smile a lot? When do you smile and why? Who do you smile most around?

Tips
- Smiling a lot is my trademark. It lets people know I am _____.
- I s_____ an average amount. There is no need to fake a s_____. I save my s_____ for my friends and family.

4 How often do you text friends/parents/partner in a day? What is the appropriate amount for each? Do you use a lot of emoji? Why or why not?

Tips
- I _____ a ton! Sometimes I _____ more than _____ times a day. It's necessary. I need to c_____ with my _____.
- I think face to face c_____ is most important so I try to limit _____.

5 What should Zac do? Please give him advice.

Tips
- Zac should tell his girlfriend and Alex about each other just so everyone is clear.
- Zac is being nice! He can have friends. He doesn't have to tell anyone.

59

Scene 9

Can you guess?

Warm-up: Survey / Ranking

🔴 **Rank how comfortable you are talking with someone new on a scale of 1 to 5.**

	NO ⟵ ⟶ YES
I like meeting new people.	1 — 2 — 3 — 4 — 5
I often talk to strangers.	1 — 2 — 3 — 4 — 5
I can easily express my feelings.	1 — 2 — 3 — 4 — 5
I like to guess about things.	1 — 2 — 3 — 4 — 5
I can easily talk with people older than me.	1 — 2 — 3 — 4 — 5

🔴 **Now share your ideas with a partner using the examples below.**

- I _____ meeting _____ people. I am _____ and learn a lot.
- I never talk with _____. I _____ to be introduced by someone.

> **Tips** like / love / old / new / strange / interested / happy / strangers / need

Can you guess? Scene 9

Reading

Read the following text.   DL 34   CD2-02

There is a little bit of Sherlock in all of us.

The great fictional detective, Sherlock Holmes, used his powers of deductive reasoning to understand people and solve cases. There is a little bit of Sherlock in all of us. We look for visual clues that are not spoken. Just think about all the things people try to understand without asking.

5   Japanese often wonder about the age of a person. There are cultural reasons for wanting to know if a person is younger or older. A person who is older will often be spoken to differently. This is not usually the case in the United States. Of course people in the USA respect their elders but the language changes little. It is impolite to ask directly, so how can we find out the age of a person we just met? Most of the
10 time, clues are given naturally in the conversation. Someone might say, "I graduated from college in 1975." Then you can just do the math.

Understanding a person's feelings may be even more difficult. Of course, non-verbal clues such as facial expression and posture may help. Tone of voice can also reveal a lot. While a shaky voice indicates nervousness, a strong and steady voice
15 shows confidence.

It can be fun making "educated guesses" when trying to make connections. If someone says that they grew up in the biggest city in New England, you would surely say, "Oh, so you are from Boston!" Making these guesses shows you are engaged in the conversation. It may even show off your knowledge of the world.

What do you think?

Share your ideas with a partner.

1. Do you consider yourself a good detective? What can you tell about a person before you ask?
2. How important is it for you to know the age of a person?
3. What are some things you should not ask or guess about?

Now, let's check out the video!

61

Let's Watch!

We meet Lily and Max for the first time.
Lily surprises Max ... more than once.

online video
online audio

 DL 35   CD2-03

What did you hear?

● **Choose exactly what each character says.**

1

A. You look a little lost.
B. You lost a little of your looks.
C. You look a little like you're lost.

2

A. I said that I'm excited more than nervous.
B. I'd say that I feel excited more than nervous.
C. I'd say that I feel nervous more than excited.

3

A. I know that I truly belong here.
B. I don't know that I truly belong here.
C. I don't know truly that I belong here.

Can you guess? Scene 9

Let's Watch! 2

Before Watching: Predict!

🔴 **Guess what the character will say.**

online video   online audio
🎧 DL 36   💿 CD2-04

A. It's the first day. Just relax!

B. Maybe you don't belong but you will.

C. Half the battle is believing you belong here.

Watch Again: Pop-up questions

online video   online audio

🔴 **Watch the whole video again and answer the questions.**

🎧 DL 35~36   💿 CD2-03   💿 CD2-04

1. What 3 things does Lily guess about Max?

2. What 3 things does Max tell Lily about himself?

3. What 3 reasons does Max give for being concerned?

4. What does Lily say Max needs to do to truly belong?

What do you think?

🔴 **Share your ideas with a partner.**

1. Do you think it is funny or strange that Lily started talking to Max before they met in class?

2. Do you think that Max should be nervous about starting classes? Give reasons.

3. Do you think Lily gave Max good advice? Give support for your answer.

63

Strategies for Improving Communication

online/video   online/audio   DL 37   CD2-05

Strategies: Note-taking

Listen and try to get the 5 main strategies from the talk. Fill in as many details as you can. After, compare with your partner.

1

2

3

4

5

Now practice with a partner using the strategies above.

Can you guess? Scene 9

 Strategies in Action

● *Practice and discuss the points in the strategy video.*

1 P_____ something about your partner. Use your senses.

Tips
• I'm guessing you _____ well last night. You look _____.
• You changed your _____ is that because you _____?

2 Choose the _____ _____ for the _____ e_____. Think about a time you tried something new. Describe how it felt. How do you feel now?

> **Tips** I felt scared/tense/elated/amazing/annoyed/bothered.

3 E_____ with how your partner felt in #2 above.

> **Tips** I remember when I … / When I had that experience … / When that happened to me … / A similar experience I had was …

4 Give some a_____. What did you think of what Lily said? Can you give a_____ or comments about the situation in #2 above?

> **Tips** I think you did the right thing … / I think you took the right course of action … / Maybe you should have tried …

5 How do you feel about calling your teacher or boss by his/her first name?

Tips
• I think it's fine if that is what my boss wants, I can do it.
• I don't feel right about it. A person in a higher position should be addressed formally.

65

Scene 10

Can we work it out?

Warm-up: Survey / Ranking

🔴 *Rank how you feel about conflict on a scale of 1 to 5.*

	NO → YES
I like to debate.	1 — 2 — 3 — 4 — 5
I often lend things to my friends.	1 — 2 — 3 — 4 — 5
I often borrow things from my friends.	1 — 2 — 3 — 4 — 5
I can easily tell my friend if I think we have a problem.	1 — 2 — 3 — 4 — 5
I can persuade a person to change his mind.	1 — 2 — 3 — 4 — 5

🔴 *Now share your ideas with a partner using the examples below.*

- I _____ borrow _____ from my friends. It only _____ to problems.
- I _____ lend things to my _____ . I am _____ to share.

Tips never / always / often / things / money / leads / family / friends / happy / sad / glad

66

Can we work it out? Scene

Reading

● **Read the following text.**

What is the best way to negotiate?

You cannot always get what you want. There are, however, times when you feel that things are not fair and you have to try to get more than you are given. What is the best way to negotiate? How can you find some middle ground that is beneficial to both parties?

The first thing to do is separate what you need from what you want. A negotiation is not a gift. It is a give and take. So keep in mind that you will have to give up something to get your desired result. Just do not let the other person know too soon what you are willing to give up.

Negotiating in good faith is also very important. If one side feels slighted, no one wins. The unhappy party will be forever looking to gain some advantage in some other way.

Preparation is the key to any good meeting. Make a list of all the things that you cannot give up and those that you are willing to compromise. Even more important might be the second list. This list should contain everything you assume the other side will and will not negotiate. If you are prepared, there is a much better chance things will go well.

Finally, never lose your cool. Keep a calm demeanor. Never let the other side see you get flustered. Just like in sports and in life, never let your emotions get the best of you.

What do you think?

● **Share your ideas with a partner.**

1. What have you had to negotiate in your life?
2. Were you ever very happy or very unhappy with the results of a negotiation?
3. What is something that you can never give up in any negotiation?

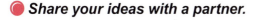
Now, let's check out the video!

Let's Watch!

Vinh has something he needs to talk about with Tim. They negotiate to find a solution.

What did you hear?

● **Choose exactly what each character says.**

1

A. I'm really spending a lot of money lately.
B. I'm really careful what I spend money on.
C. I'm not so careful what I spend money on.

2

A. I don't even eat that much, because I can't.
B. I don't even go out that much, because I can't.
C. I don't even eat out that much, because I can't.

3

A. I was thinking how much food costs.
B. I was thinking that maybe we could share the food.
C. I was thinking that maybe we could share the food costs.

Can we work it out?   Scene 10

Let's Watch! 2

Before Watching: Predict!

● **Guess what the character will say.**

DL 40   CD2-08

A. I don't think so. I never eat your food.

B. I don't know. I mean you do eat all my leftover Indian food.

C. I think that would be a great idea. How much do I owe you?

Watch Again: Pop-up questions

● **Watch the whole video again and answer the questions.**

DL 39~40   CD2-07   CD2-08

1. What are 2 ways Vinh saves money?

___

2. Name 2 reasons that Vinh gives for eating Tim's food?

___

3. What else does Vinh borrow from Tim and why?

___

4. What does Tim agree to do?

___

What do you think?

● **Share your ideas with a partner.**

1. How do you think this problem started?

2. Does Tim understand his own problems? Give examples.

3. How do you think this all could have been prevented? Give a possible solution.

69

Strategies for Improving Communication

 DL 41 CD2-09

Strategies: Note-taking

Listen and try to get the 5 main strategies from the talk. Fill in as many details as you can. After, compare with your partner.

1

2

3

4

5

Now practice with a partner using the strategies above.

Can we work it out? Scene

 Strategies in Action

🔴 *Try role playing the situation in scene 10. One student is Tim and the other is Vinh. Do not copy the scene exactly. Try to not use any notes when acting.*

Tim is eating Vinh's food. Start.

1. Say something p_____.

   Tips I really like … / I love the way you … / You know, you are really good at …

2. T_____. This is set but make sure you are standing up when you do this exercise.

   Tips I see that you are … now. / I could not help but notice you are … now.

3. Ask q_____ to see how Tim feels and debates.

   Tips Did you ever notice how I/you …? / Do you realize that you …?

4. Suggest a possible s_____.

   Tips Do you think it might be possible to …? / What if we …? / How about we try …?

5. Make the d_____.

   Tips So it's a d_____? / I will … and you …, right? / So we have agreed to …, right? Great!

Now try the strategies with a different situation. Vinh can't sleep/ concentrate because Tim is making too much noise.

1. Stay _____.

2. Tim is singing loudly or playing guitar. / Tim's friends never leave.

3. Vinh might say: You know I have to wake early for classes/do homework?

4. S_____. What if we had a two-hour quiet time each night? / Would you mind _____? / Do you think we might try _____?

5. Tim counters with: OK, but you gotta join my band! / You have to study in the library three nights a week!

Now make your own ideas for: Vinh is always washing Tim's dirty dishes.

71

Scene 11

How do you describe events?

 ### Warm-up: Survey / Ranking

🔴 **Rank your taste and how easily you trust others on a scale of 1 to 5.**

	NO ⬅ ➡ YES
I like hiking and the outdoors.	1 — 2 — 3 — 4 — 5
I remember details easily.	1 — 2 — 3 — 4 — 5
I like to go to expensive restaurants.	1 — 2 — 3 — 4 — 5
My best days are spent with just one friend.	1 — 2 — 3 — 4 — 5
I can have a great day without spending money.	1 — 2 — 3 — 4 — 5

🔴 **Now share your ideas with a partner using the examples below.**

- The best days I can _____ are spent with _____ _____ . I like to be in a _____ .

- I can remember every _____ of my _____ days. They all seem like _____ .

> **Tips** group / detail / many / yesterday / friends / remember / favorite

How do you describe events? Scene 11

Reading

● **Read the following text.**

DL 42   CD2-10

The best day ever

Imagine your favorite day. Can you recall all the details? Can you explain to your friends why that day was so fantastic? The more you remember, the better you will be able to share your experience. Days can usually be remembered by where you went, what you did, what you ate, and who you were with.

5   Most perfect days start with getting up early and getting out of the house. I like to head to the beach just after sunrise with a friend. Of course the connection has to be there. That person has to love the beach too!

Then you think about what there is to do. I love big waves. I'm not a surfer but I bodysurf 1-2 meter waves. Sometimes I get smashed into the sand but that is all 10   part of the thrill. For me, the beach is a sport. For it to be a perfect day, my friend has to be out in the ocean trying to catch the waves with me. I like to snorkel too and if I am lucky I can see sea turtles and dolphins swimming in the distance.

Eating is a huge part of a perfect day for most people but I am happy with a couple of mangoes from the nearest tree.

15   Finally, you have to be able to describe the day, so try using all five senses so that others can get a vivid picture of exactly how it felt. If you do it right, they will feel as if they were there too!

What do you think?

● **Share your ideas with a partner.**

1. Can you describe your favorite day? Where did you go? What did you do?
2. Who do you usually spend your best days with? Why do you think so?
3. How many of the five senses can you use to describe your day?

Now, let's check out the video!

Let's Watch!

Alex and Jenny are now roommates! Alex is excited about her great day out. Jenny, however, has a few questions.

online / video
online / audio
DL 43   CD2-11

What did you hear?

● **Choose exactly what each character says.**

1

A. That's surprisingly nice.
B. That's a nice surprise.
C. That's nicely surprising.

2

A. Once we got there, there weren't many people there.
B. Once we got there, there were so many people there.
C. Once we got there, there weren't so many people there.

3

A. Then he made Italian sandwiches.
B. Then he made real Italian sandwiches.
C. Then he really made Italian sandwiches.

How do you describe events?   Scene 11

Let's Watch! 2

Before Watching: Predict!

● **Guess what the character will say.**

online video   online audio

🎧 DL 44   💿 CD2-12

A. You believe everything.

B. You should believe him.

C. Seeing is believing. Did you see him making them?

Watch Again: Pop-up questions

online video   online audio

● **Watch the whole video again and answer the questions.**

🎧 DL 43~44   💿 CD2-11   💿 CD2-12

1. Where did Alex go with Zac? Be specific.

_____

2. Why were there so few people there?

_____

3. What was in the food Zac brought?

_____

4. What is Zac's job?

_____

What do you think?

● **Share your ideas with a partner.**

1. Do you think Zac made the sandwiches? Why or why not?

2. Why do you think Jenny did not say more about Zac?

3. Do you think this sounds like a good date? Give reasons.

75

Strategies for Improving Communication

Strategies: Note-taking

Listen and try to get the 3 main strategies from the talk. Fill in as many details as you can. After, compare with your partner.

1.

2.

3.

Now practice with a partner using the strategies above.

How do you describe events?   Scene 11

Strategies in Action

🔴 *Take a memo of your thoughts on each point. After, you will be interviewed by a partner.*

1 Name 3 things you like to do and why.

-
-
-

Tips
- I love _____. It makes me feel _____.
- One of my favorite things to do is _____. It is _____ but it makes me _____.

2 Name 2 n_____ things you really want to do.

-
-

Tips
- I've always wanted to _____.
- Just once in my life I want to try _____ because _____.
- _____ is on my list of things to do.

3 Describe 2 kinds of f_____ you like. Use your senses.

-
-

Tips
- I think _____ is the most beautiful f_____. It looks like _____.
- I love the smell of _____. It is so _____.
- I love the taste of _____. It melts in my mouth.

Now describe your ideal day out. Mention at least 3 things to do. Give more reasons and details if you can.

Tips My perfect day would start at _____ and we would _____. Then _____ in the afternoon before finally _____.

77

Scene 12

What are you into?

◆ Warm-up: Survey / Ranking

🔴 **Rank how open you are to change on a scale of 1 to 5.**

	NO ⇦ ⇨ YES
I like to challenge myself by trying new things.	1 — 2 — 3 — 4 — 5
I have a good way to get rid of stress.	1 — 2 — 3 — 4 — 5
It is important to be comfortable.	1 — 2 — 3 — 4 — 5
Pain is sometimes necessary.	1 — 2 — 3 — 4 — 5
I want to improve my mind and body.	1 — 2 — 3 — 4 — 5

🔴 **Now share your ideas with a partner using the examples below.**

- I play _____ so _____ is necessary to get better. I need to _____ myself.

- Relaxing is most _____ to me. Pain only causes me more stress.

> **Tips** tennis / practice / important / challenge / improve / fun

What are you into? Scene

Reading

● **Read the following text.**

Passion—What shapes the way you look at the world?

What really wakes you up in the morning? I'm not talking about your alarm clock or a place you are forced to go. If you had nothing to do all day, what excites you enough to get out of bed? For many people it is a hobby and if you are fortunate, it is more; it is a passion. If you have a passion then you need to be able to communicate it to others.

5　Start from the beginning. Can you remember who first got you interested in it? Was it an older sibling, a parent, or a teacher? How old were you when you first fell in love with it? Is it something that you want to pass on to others? If so, then think about how and why.

　Something you are passionate about shapes the way you look at the world. It could
10　be the lyrics from your favorite musician, a work of art you saw in a museum, a sport you play, or a video game. Think about the ways it has taught you about the world you live in. Are there rules or lessons from your hobby that have become your rules in life?

　So what can you do to find your passion if you have not yet? The answer is simple:
15　try something new every day. You need to keep reading and researching but more importantly, you need to be trying things. Life is short, so there is no reason to wait. Get out there and do it!

What do you think?

● **Share your ideas with a partner.**

1. Do you have a hobby that changed your life?
2. How did you become interested in your current hobbies?
3. What is something new that you want to try?

> Now, let's check out the video!

Let's Watch!

Maya meets Kate by the river.
Kate explains that yoga is more than just a hobby.

DL 47   CD2-15

What did you hear? ● *Choose exactly what each character says.*

1
A. Do you mind if I ask you a question?
B. Did you mind if I ask you a question?
C. Do you mind if I asked you a question?

2
A. It energizes me and helps me to heal.
B. It energized me and helps me to heal.
C. It will energize me and help me to heal.

3
A. So, if I were to do this, right now, I would feel good too?
B. So, if I were to do that, right now, I would feel good too?
C. So, if I were to do that, right now, I would have felt good too?

What are you into? Scene 12

Let's Watch! 2

Before Watching: Predict!

online video   online audio

● **Guess what the character will say.**   DL 48   CD2-16

A. It's the first day. Just relax!

B. You most certainly could not do this right now.

C. You would absolutely feel better if you did this now.

Watch Again: Pop-up questions

online video   online audio

● **Watch the whole video again and answer the questions.**

DL 47~48   CD2-15   CD2-16

1. What does Kate say about modern life?

   _____

2. What 3 things does Kate say yoga helps her to focus on?

   _____

3. What are 2 things that Kate says will happen to your mind after practicing yoga?

   _____

4. What does Maya say that she has some trouble with?

   _____

What do you think?

● **Share your ideas with a partner.**

1. What do you think are the biggest causes of stress in modern life?

2. What do you think are the best ways to get rid of stress?

3. Do you think you would like to try yoga? Why or why not?

81

Strategies for Improving Communication

online video   online audio   🎧 DL 49   ⊙ CD2-17

Strategies: Note-taking

Listen and try to get the 5 main strategies from the talk. Fill in as many details as you can. After, compare with your partner.

1
2
3
4
5

Now practice with a partner using the strategies above.

What are you into? Scene 12

 Strategies in Action

🔴 *Take a memo of your thoughts on each strategy point then share with a partner.*

1 Tell w_____ you like your hobby and how it makes you feel. What benefit does it give you?

> **Tips**
> - I like _____ because it makes me feel _____.
> - It makes me stronger/smarter/more international/interesting/energetic/skilled.

2 Tell when you started and why. Are there levels?

> **Tips**
> - I started playing baseball/basketball/piano/surfing when I was six/eight/in elementary school/living in America.
> - My mother/father/grandmother/grandfather taught me how.
> - There are many levels. I'm a brown belt now but I'll be a black belt in a few years.

3 How does it _____ into your _____ or society?

> **Tips**
> - Sports have clear rules. You know when you win or lose. Society is different.
> - Movies help me understand the world but also to escape reality.

4 Tell what others might not like about your hobby.

> **Tips**
> - It takes hours of practice every day. It's really hard.
> - Baseball can be boring.
> - I get bloody playing rugby. It's pretty dangerous and you get dirty.

5 Ask 3-4 questions when listening to your partner. Show you are interested.

> **Tips**
> - Were you always good or did it take time?
> - Did you ever get hurt?
> - What do you learn from it?
> - What was your best memory?
> - How does it help you in your daily life?

Scene 13

How do you help a friend?

Warm-up: Survey / Ranking

🔴 **Rank your emotional awareness on a scale of 1 to 5.**

	NO ⟵⟶ YES
I often cheer up my friends.	1 — 2 — 3 — 4 — 5
My friends often cheer me up.	1 — 2 — 3 — 4 — 5
I can easily read my friend's emotions.	1 — 2 — 3 — 4 — 5
I am not very good at hiding my feelings.	1 — 2 — 3 — 4 — 5
I like it when my friends tell me their problems.	1 — 2 — 3 — 4 — 5

🔴 **Now share your ideas with a partner using the examples below.**

- Cheering up my friend makes me very _____. I want them to understand they are _____ to me.

- My friends always _____ me up. When I am feeling _____, I go _____ with my friend.

> **Tips** happy / energy / excited / important / cheers / low / down / out

84

Reading

Read the following text.

More a true friendship than a fan club

What is a friend? This is very hard to define as there are many different kinds of friendships. Some are working friendships, some are situational, and others come about because of shared interests. We know that friends support each other. Friends are there when we need them and some seem to know you better than you know yourself.

Secrets are something friends share because there is trust. If you value your friendships then surely you can keep a secret to yourself. Friends also share information because they might be looking for advice. A good friend will be honest even if it means saying something the other person does not want to hear. If you always agree with your friend it is probably more a fan club than a true friendship.

So be there when your friend needs you and, sure, you can tell your friend to "look on the bright side," but it would be even better if you can show where the bright side has been hiding. If your friend is in the dark, then you have to bring the light and remind her what is good.

Think about your best friend. Is that person someone who challenges you when you are doing something wrong or someone who always agrees? Hopefully, your best friend is someone who makes you a better person.

What do you think?

Share your ideas with a partner.

1. Who is your best friend and why?
2. Are you good at keeping secrets? Can you give an example?
3. How do you cheer your friend up? What have you done or said to make your friend feel better?

Now, let's check out the video!

Let's Watch!

Lily meets Josh after a long time. Josh, being a good friend, does his best to make her feel better.

online/video
online/audio

🎧 DL 51   💿 CD2-19

What did you hear?

● **Choose exactly what each character says.**

1
A. I get pretty good at reading that face.
B. I'll get pretty good at reading that face.
C. I've gotten pretty good at reading that face.

2

A. He works all the time and when I do get to see him, he's tired.
B. When he works all the time and I do get to see him, he's tired.
C. He's tired all the time and when I do get to see him, he will be working.

3

A. It means he works 24/7.
B. It means he works 24 hours.
C. It means he works 7 days a week.

How do you help a friend?   Scene 13

Let's Watch! 2

Before Watching: Predict!

● **Guess what the character will say.**

DL 52   CD2-20

A. Awesome. I can't wait to see it!

B. Right. Sorry I'm too busy to see it!

C. You are directing a play? I didn't know that!

Watch Again: Pop-up questions

● **Watch the whole video again and answer the questions.**

DL 51~52   CD2-19   CD2-20

1. How does Josh know that Lily is sad?

___

2. What 2 things make Lily busy?

___

3. Does Josh say something bad about Zac? What does he say?

___

4. What does Josh agree to at the end?

___

What do you think?

● **Share your ideas with a partner.**

1. Why do you think Zac does not make enough time for Lily?

2. Do you agree with Josh that it is "tough to watch" public displays of affection? Or do you agree with Lily?

3. Do you think that it is OK to make work more important than relationships? Why or why not?

Strategies for Improving Communication

 DL 53   CD2-21

Strategies: Note-taking

Listen and try to get the 5 main strategies from the talk. Fill in as many details as you can. After, compare with your partner.

1.

2.

3.

4.

5.

Now practice with a partner using the strategies above.

How do you help a friend?   Scene

 Strategies in Action

🔴 *Make up a story or choose one from below so you can practice the strategies with a partner.*

▪ Your best friend has no more time anymore, so you are lonely.
▪ You keep making mistakes at work and the boss is not nice.
▪ Your parents treat you like a high school student. Your curfew is much too early.

1 Use p_____ and n_____ intonation saying the same words. Just like Lily does when she first says, "I'm great …."

> **Tips** Everything is fabulous. / I'm so happy. / I've never been better. / I'm living the dream.

2 F_____ e_____. Use them. Have fun making them.

> **Tips**
> • smile / frown / interested / confused / angry …
> • Try different posture too. straight up / lean in / slouch / lean back.

3 Take a guess at what the problem might be.

> **Tips**
> • I know the problem, you just _____.
> • Your teacher is giving you too much homework?
> • Your parents told you to come home early again tonight?
> • Your boss scolded you again?

4 Take a _____ but appreciate both _____.

> **Tips**
> • Well, you do live with your parents, so you have to follow their rules. Maybe you can compromise. Go out less but stay out longer each time.

5 Don't just a _____. Try showing the other side of the story.

> **Tips**
> • I know your boss is mean but you'll get better. If you concentrate, you won't make mistakes, right?

Scene 14

What are you talking about?

Warm-up: Survey / Ranking

🔴 **Rank how direct you prefer conversation on a scale of 1 to 5.**

	NO ⬅ ➡ YES
I can tell if someone is lying to me.	1 — 2 — 3 — 4 — 5
If I know someone is lying, I tell them right away.	1 — 2 — 3 — 4 — 5
I can control my emotions very well.	1 — 2 — 3 — 4 — 5
I get to the point quickly if I have an issue with another person.	1 — 2 — 3 — 4 — 5
Speaking directly is not my strong point.	1 — 2 — 3 — 4 — 5

🔴 **Now share your ideas with a partner using the examples below.**

- I think it is _____ to speak directly. It saves _____ and _____.
  Communication _____ be clear.
- Sometimes a _____ lie is _____. It can avoid _____ someone.

> **Tips** good / time / energy / must / should / OK / small / hurting

What are you talking about? Scene 14

Reading

● **Read the following text.**

Avoiding miscommunication

We have been looking at how to make connections. The key has been in putting your thoughts and feelings into words but sometimes this is difficult. There are times when you are not sure how you feel, or even worse yet, you speak after being given bad information. We have to take a look at how to avoid this kind of situation and miscommunication.

It was said that the Roman emperor Tiberius never said anything to anyone without writing it down first. While the validity of this is debatable, the idea behind it is sound. It is always better to gather your thoughts before saying anything rash. How many times have you quickly replied to an email or text and wish you had taken more time?

It is also essential to be sure that you have the proper information before having a discussion. This can be difficult with the onslaught of unedited material on the internet. If you need material to support your opinion, the internet is most likely your most valuable tool. Make sure you know how to use it, though. All sources are not the same. Learn which are trustworthy.

When it comes to friends, understand that everyone has their own point of view. Try talking to all the people involved before taking a side. This can be hard because emotions can run hot. When this happens, try taking advice from the second emperor of Rome. You have the ability to control time. Use it to your advantage.

What do you think?

● **Share your ideas with a partner.**

1. Have you ever sent a text that you regretted?
2. Are you good at processing information? Do you know what sources are good or questionable?
3. How good are you at controlling your emotions? Have you ever lost your temper?

Now, let's check out the video!

Let's Watch!

Zac meets Alex's new roommate, Jenny, in the park again. This time, she is not so happy with him, but is she right?

DL 55   CD2-23

What did you hear?

● **Choose exactly what each character says.**

1
A. Change is the only constant.
B. Only change is the constant.
C. Change is constantly changing.

2
A. I made some time at seeing theater with Lily.
B. I made some time for seeing theater with Lily.
C. I'll make some time for seeing theater with Lily.

3
A. She probably felt like a kid.
B. She probably felt like kidding.
C. She'll probably feel like a kid.

What are you talking about?   Scene 14

Let's Watch! 2

Before Watching: Predict!

● **Guess what the character will say.**

online video   online audio

🎧 DL 56   ⊙ CD2-24

A. Yes, it's double-parked.
B. No, I don't have a car.
C. How did you know I had a car?

Watch Again: Pop-up questions

online video   online audio

● **Watch the whole video again and answer the questions.**

🎧 DL 55~56   ⊙ CD2-23   ⊙ CD2-24

1. What 4 things has Zac been doing this summer?

2. What 5 things does Zac like about the beach?

3. What does Jenny say about her roommate Alex? Give 2 examples.

4. What is one thing that we now know that Zac lied about?

What do you think?

● **Share your ideas with a partner.**

1. Do you think Zac is a bad guy or just misunderstood?

2. Where in the conversation do you think things could have been cleared up if someone said something different?

3. Do you think Zac is being treated unfairly by Jenny? Give reasons.

Strategies for Improving Communication

online video　online audio　🎧 DL 57　💿 CD2-25

Strategies: Note-taking

Listen and try to get the 5 main strategies from the talk. Fill in as many details as you can. After, compare with your partner.

1.

2.

3.

4.

5.

Now practice with a partner using the strategies above.

What are you talking about? Scene

Strategies in Action

● *See how the conversation could be improved. What could Zac or Jenny have said differently?*

1 Take a look at the scene video and see how it could improve the conversation.

Jenny: I was thinking about you last week, not so much since.
Zac: OK, so, how's your summer been?

Instead he could have said _____.

Zac: Do I know her?
Jenny: Maybe. I'm not sure yet.

Instead she could have said _____.

Jenny: Do you know where I can get good Italian sandwiches?

Instead she could have said _____.

2 Practice saying what Jenny says but using different emotions. Don't be angry.

Tips Why do you love the beach, Zac? / Is your car double-parked? / Could you hold this for me? I want to test something. / I'm OK. Are you OK?

3 Zac needed to c_____ why Jenny was saying what she was saying. Could you name other points where Zac could have c_____ what Jenny was saying? For example, "Why are you asking me about sandwiches?" or "What is your roommate's name?"

4 Practice an e_____ s_____.

Tips Well, I'd better be going. / Look at the time! I'm late. / I have a movie to catch. / Time flies when you are having fun … thank you but I must go.

5 Of course, Never p_____. Discuss when you think Zac may have p_____.

Tips
- I think Zac might have panicked when _____.
- I thought Zac was going to panic when _____.

95

Scene 15

Can you tell me a story?

Warm-up: Survey / Ranking

🔴 **Rank how you feel about storytelling on a scale of 1 to 5.**

	NO ⬅ ➡ YES
I am a good listener.	1 — 2 — 3 — 4 — 5
I like when my friends tell me stories.	1 — 2 — 3 — 4 — 5
I know how to tell a great story.	1 — 2 — 3 — 4 — 5
I think storytelling is very important.	1 — 2 — 3 — 4 — 5
I remember details when telling a story.	1 — 2 — 3 — 4 — 5

🔴 **Now share your ideas with a partner using the examples below.**

- I love stories. My _____ tells the best stories. I can almost _____ I am there.

- Some stories _____ too long. I wish people _____ get to the _____.

Tips ▶ friend / mother / father / believe / feel / last / go / would / should / point

Reading

Read the following text.

Telling stories—The desire to share information and experience

Telling stories is one of the most important skills of communication, indeed, of what it means to be human. It has been part of the human experience for at least 40,000 years, when ancient hunters drew pictures on caves. A desire then, to share information and experience— the desire to "connect"— is not so different from what we do today. Telling a story can also help someone to understand something they have yet to do.

Humans share the experience of being human but we all see things from a different point of view. Some people are educated and some are not. There are people who travel all around the world and a few that have never left their hometown. A good story will appeal, on some level though, to everyone. Shakespeare understood this well. He wrote in a time when many people could not even read. Still, he was popular with all types of people because he had characters and situations in his plays that reached his audience intellectually and emotionally. He knew that a great story reaches the heart and the mind.

If we look at the more recent past, movies and television are trying to do similar things today. Things are more technologically advanced but the goal is the same.

Everyone has stories and, with the internet, it has never been easier to share your story. You do not need a big budget. You can just talk into the camera and upload it. The world has never been more connected.

What do you think?

Share your ideas with a partner.

1. Are you a good storyteller? Can you give an example?
2. Do you listen or read stories often? What movies have you seen recently?
3. Do you ever upload your stories to the internet? What are they usually about?

Now, let's check out the video!

Let's Watch!

Maya tells Kate a story.
Kate is interested from start to finish.

online / video
online / audio

DL 59   CD2-27

What did you hear?

● Choose exactly what each character says.

1

A. Do you know what happens if you cut the cord?
B. You do know what happens if you cut the cord?
C. Do you know that happens when you cut the cord?

2

A. Where you watching?
B. What were you watching?
C. When were you watching?

3

A. I need to find it so it's true.
B. I need to find out if it's true.
C. I need to find out if it's truth.

Can you tell me a story? Scene 15

Let's Watch! 2

Before Watching: Predict!

● **Guess what the character will say.**

online video   online audio   DL 60   CD2-28

A. And I started glowing like a lamp.
B. And I got thrown back like two meters.
C. And then, there was silence. Nothing really happened.

Watch Again: Pop-up questions

online video   online audio

● **Watch the whole video again and answer the questions.**

DL 59~60   CD2-27   CD2-28

1. What was Maya watching that made her think to cut the cord?

2. Describe the scissors.

3. What 3 questions did Maya's mother ask?

4. What does Maya say "… is a dangerous thing?"

What do you think?

● **Share your ideas with a partner.**

1. Why do you think children do dangerous things even when they know it is wrong?
2. Why do you think Maya's mother did not get angry?
3. What did you think of Maya's story? Do you have any similar stories?

Strategies for Improving Communication

  DL 61 CD2-29

Strategies: Note-taking

Listen and try to get the 5 main strategies from the talk. Fill in as many details as you can. After, compare with your partner.

1.

2.

3.

4.

5.

Now practice with a partner using the strategies above.

Can you tell me a story? Scene 15

Strategies in Action

🔴 *Now it's time for you to tell a story.*

1 _____. Find the right time.

> **Tips** That reminds me … / Do you have 5 minutes? / There is something I really have to tell you. / Are you busy now?

2 The c_____. How do you make the listener interested?

> **Tips** Did you ever _____? / Have you ever tried _____? / Remember when we _____? Well, I have a new story about that!

3 B_____ the story. Make sure you have a beginning, middle, and end.

> **Tips** First _____. After that we _____. Finally, we went to the _____ and _____.

4 D_____. Make sure you talk about the setting and use adjectives.

> **Tips**
> Setting:
> Time: night / day / very early morning.
> Place: it was dark and scary / new and charming.
> Conditions: it was really sunny / dark and rainy.

5 R_____. What can we learn from the story?

> **Tips**
> • So the lesson from this is never/always _____.
> • So the moral of the story is _____.

このテキストのメインページ
www.kinsei-do.co.jp/plusmedia/4076

次のページのQRコードを読み取ると直接ページにジャンプできます

オンライン映像配信サービス「plus⁺Media」について

本テキストの映像と音声は plus⁺Media ページ（www.kinsei-do.co.jp/plusmedia）から、ストリーミング再生でご利用いただけます。手順は以下に従ってください。

ログイン

- ●ご利用には、ログインが必要です。
  サイトのログインページ（www.kinsei-do.co.jp/plusmedia/login）へ行き、plus⁺Media パスワード（次のページのシールをはがしたあとに印字されている数字とアルファベット）を入力します。

- ●パスワードは各テキストにつき1つです。
  有効期限は、はじめてログインした時点から1年間になります。

ログインページ

[利用方法]

次のページにあるQRコード、もしくは plus⁺Media トップページ（www.kinsei-do.co.jp/plusmedia）から該当するテキストを選んで、そのテキストのメインページにジャンプしてください。

plus+Media トップ　　メインページ

メニューページ　　再生画面

「Video」「Audio」をタッチすると、それぞれのメニューページにジャンプしますので、そこから該当する項目を選べば、ストリーミングが開始されます。

[推奨環境]

iOS (iPhone, iPad)	OS: iOS 6 〜 12　ブラウザ：標準ブラウザ	Android	OS: Android 4.x 〜 8.0　ブラウザ：標準ブラウザ、Chrome
PC	OS: Windows 7/8/8.1/10, MacOS X	ブラウザ: Internet Explorer 10/11, Microsoft Edge, Firefox 48以降, Chrome 53以降, Safari		

※最新の推奨環境についてはウェブサイトをご確認ください。
※上記の推奨環境を満たしている場合でも、機種によってはご利用いただけない場合もあります。また、推奨環境は技術動向等により変更される場合があります。予めご了承ください。

本書には CD（別売）があります

Finding Connections
―Communication and Culture in 15 Scenes―

15のシーンで学ぶ
つながるための英語コミュニケーション！

2019年1月20日　初版第1刷発行
2023年8月25日　初版第5刷発行

著　者　　Todd Rucynski

発行者　　福　岡　正　人
発行所　　株式会社　金星堂

（〒101-0051）東京都千代田区神田神保町 3-21
Tel.（03）3263-3828（営業部）
　　（03）3263-3997（編集部）
Fax（03）3263-0716
https://www.kinsei-do.co.jp

編集担当　今門貴浩・長島吉成　　　　　Printed in Japan
印刷所・製本所／大日本印刷株式会社

本書の無断複製・複写は著作権法上での例外を除き禁じられています。
本書を代行業者等の第三者に依頼してスキャンやデジタル化すること
は、たとえ個人や家庭内での利用であっても認められておりません。
落丁・乱丁本はお取り替えいたします。

ISBN978-4-7647-4076-1　C1082